Grace...Pace...Space. So ran one of the best-known motoring slogans of all time; and better than anything else, it sums up the qualities which made Jaguar a legend. From their origins in the Swallow Sidecar Company, through their early days as SS cars, to the emergence of the famous Jaguar name in 1936, there has always been a certain magic associated with Jaguar cars; a *marque* which has almost always competed in looks with the most elegant; which has usually competed with the fastest; and which has often competed in comfort and finish with the most luxurious; all whilst still remaining a realistic ambition for those who could not hope to afford a Mercedes Benz SSK, a Gurney Nutting low-chassis Daimler, a Rolls Royce, or a Ferrari. It is with such cars as these that Jaguar must be compared.

Apart from their undoubted qualities as road-going cars, Jaguar, in both saloon and sports car form, have excelled on the world's major racing tracks. Few *marques* can boast of such success as enjoyed by the legendary competition C and D types: of the five D types entered at Le Mans in 1957 all were to finish, taking five of the first six places. In saloon car competitions, the classic Mark II proved all but unbeatable with its devastating acceleration, superb handling and excellent power output.

Today, having taken over from the exquisite E type, it is the sophisticated XJ-S that has taken up the challenge and, with the recent announcement that Jaguar Cars Limited are to once more become involved in competition, it is surely only a matter of time before the "big cats" repeat the successes of the past.

BRON KOWAL

The Jaguar name first appeared in 1936 on a re-designed model range produced by S.S. Cars Ltd. The name had been introduced to distinguish the new, higher-performance product from its somewhat pedestrian – if excitingly-styled – predecessors. Thanks to the work of Harry Weslake and William Heynes, the performance from these new, but still Standard powered, cars was considerably improved. Shown on *these pages* is a 1937 SS 100 fitted with a straight-6 engine of 2.5 litre capacity. The following year the same model was offered with a 3.5 litre engine producing 125 bhp and a top speed in excess of 100 mph.

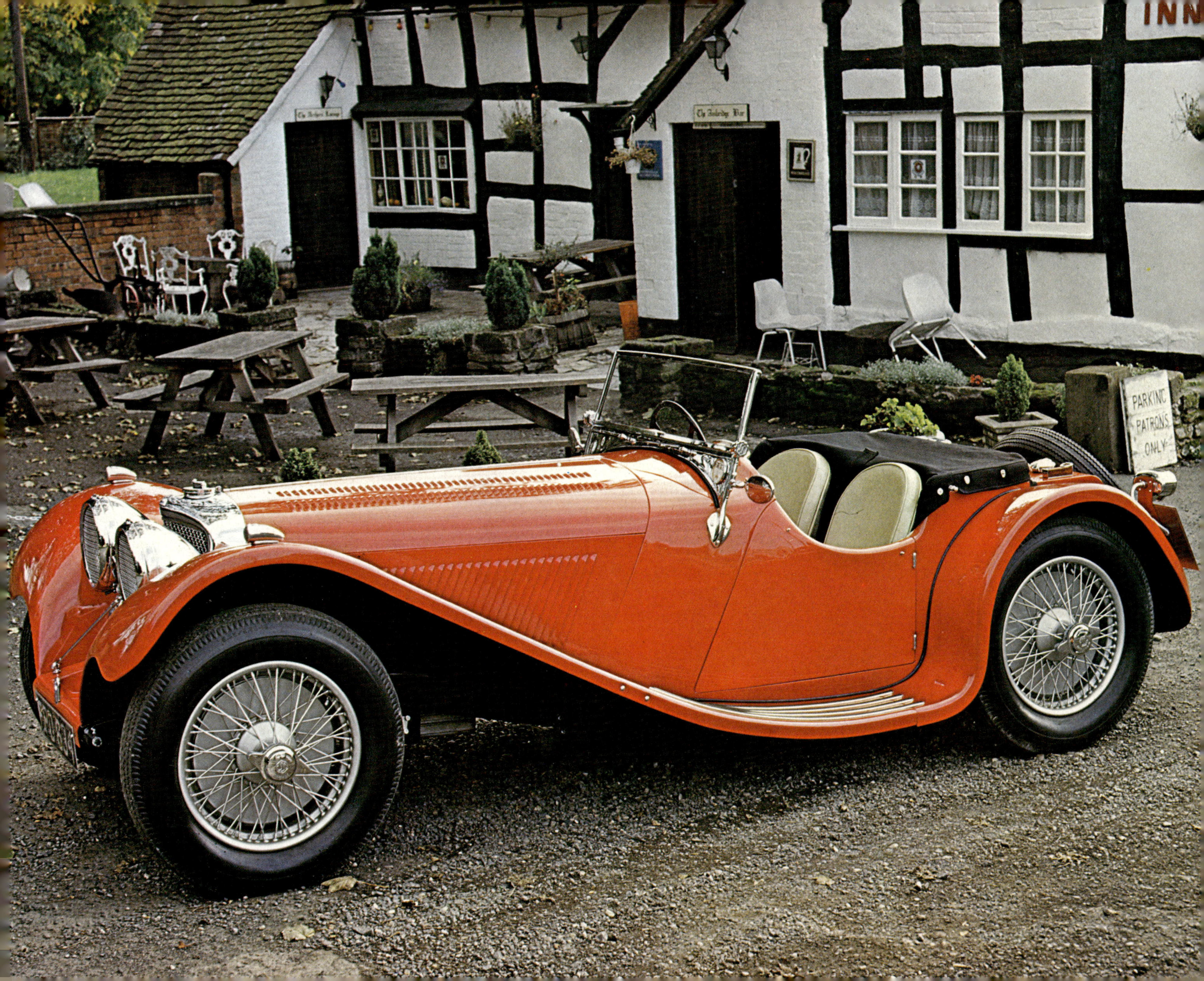
INN
PARKINC
PATRONS
ONLY

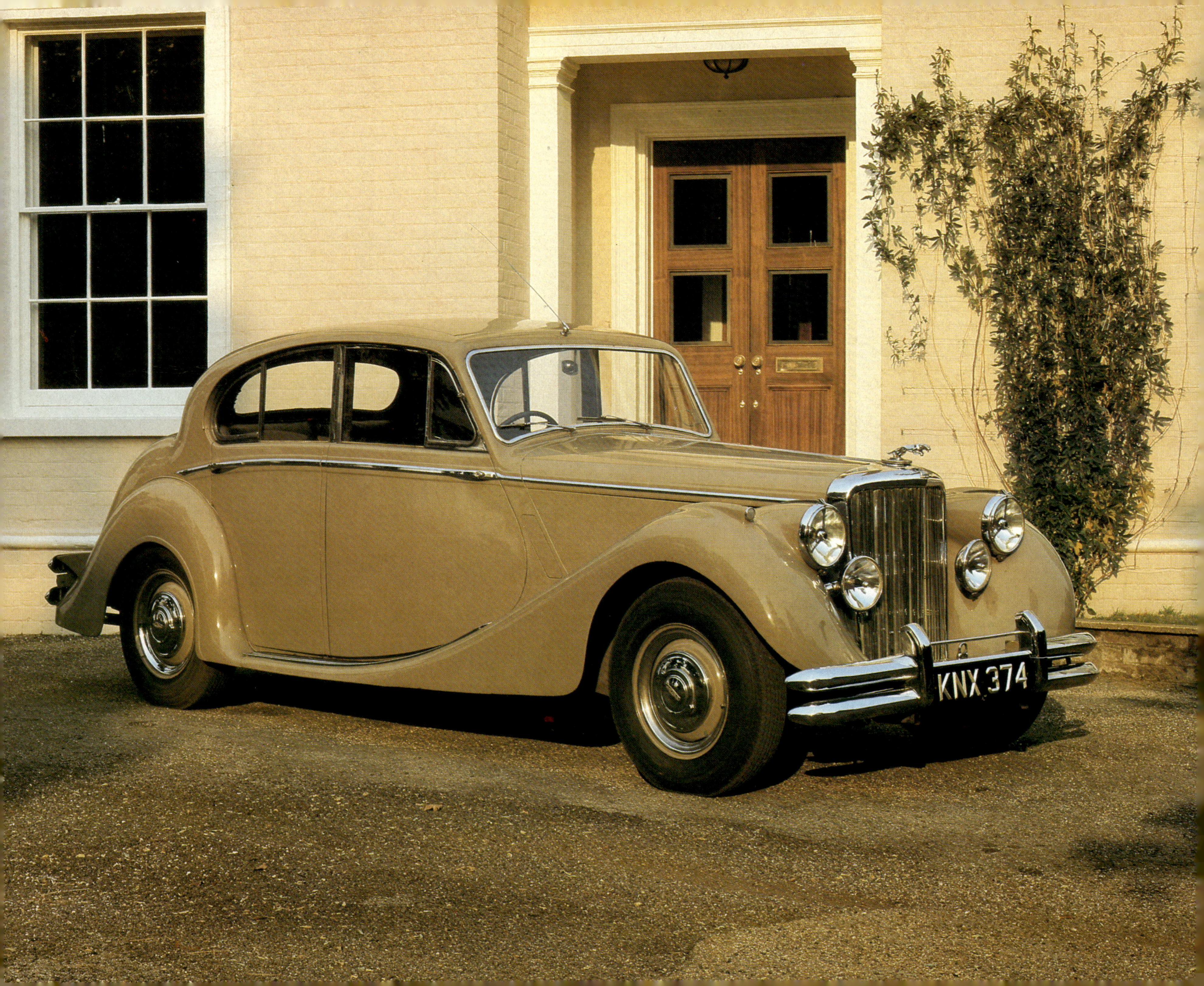
KNX 374

After the war the company name was changed to Jaguar Cars Ltd. and the SS designation discontinued. The acclaimed SS 100, which was later to be referred to as the Mark IV, was dropped from the range, and in its place came the stop-gap Mark V. This used the chassis that had been developed for the proposed Mark VII, and was available with the old 2.6 and 3.5 litre 6 cylinder engines. Pictured on *these pages* is a 1950 3.5 litre 4-door saloon version of the elegant Mark V.

In 1948 the sensational XK120 was announced to an eager motoring fraternity. Powered by the first true Jaguar engine, a straight-6 of 3442 cc with twin overhead camshafts, the car soon proved its worth in competitions. The 1954 XK140 *these pages* was a modified version of the XK120 with improved weight-distribution, a close-ratio gearbox, and a number of other improvements.

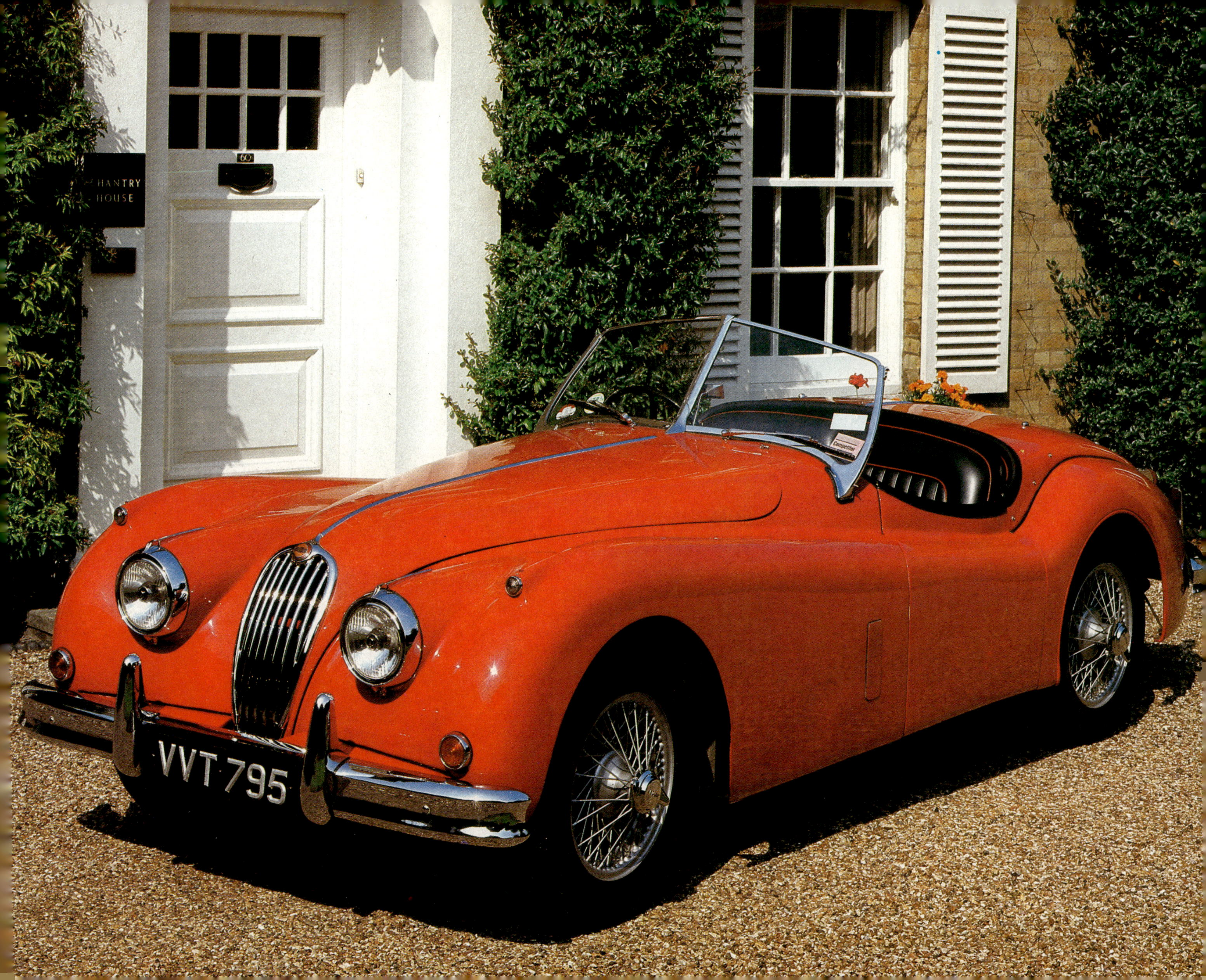
VVT 795

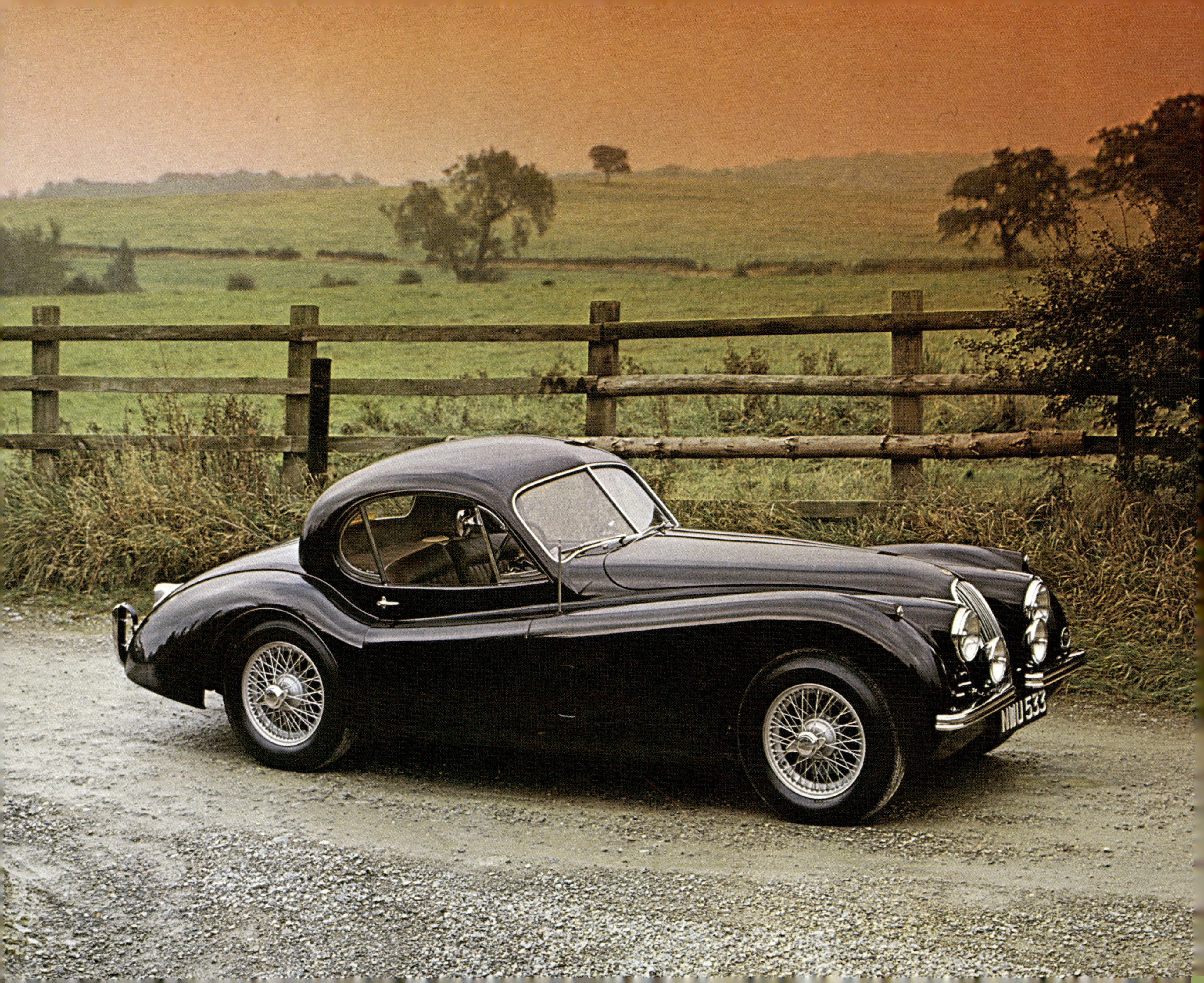

Pictured *these pages* is a 1954 XK120 fixed-head coupé. Externally, the car can be distinguished from the XK140 by the bumpers and the radiator grille design. Early models of the 120 were aluminium bodied but in 1950, when it was obvious that demand for the car was going to be considerable, an all-steel body was fitted. The XK120 was more than just a good performer with an exciting body shape. As can be seen from the shot of its interior, it blended these essential characteristics with a high degree of luxury and driver comfort.

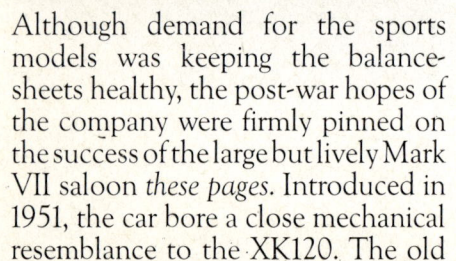

Although demand for the sports models was keeping the balance-sheets healthy, the post-war hopes of the company were firmly pinned on the success of the large but lively Mark VII saloon *these pages*. Introduced in 1951, the car bore a close mechanical resemblance to the XK120. The old pushrod engine that had powered the Mark V was discarded in favour of the acclaimed twin cam unit which gave this large saloon a top speed of 103 mph. With its unique combination of size, luxury, performance and low price this model knew no peers.

The C type Jaguar which
outstanding success. In
performance, the compa
pages. That same year, o
entered in the race and

In 1966 the 2+2 fixed head model *these pages* was introduced. The wheelbase was lengthened by 9 inches and the roofline raised to allow for the extra seating at the rear. Still referred to as a series I, this model was now offered with an automatic gearbox. Roadster and coupé designs remained unchanged.

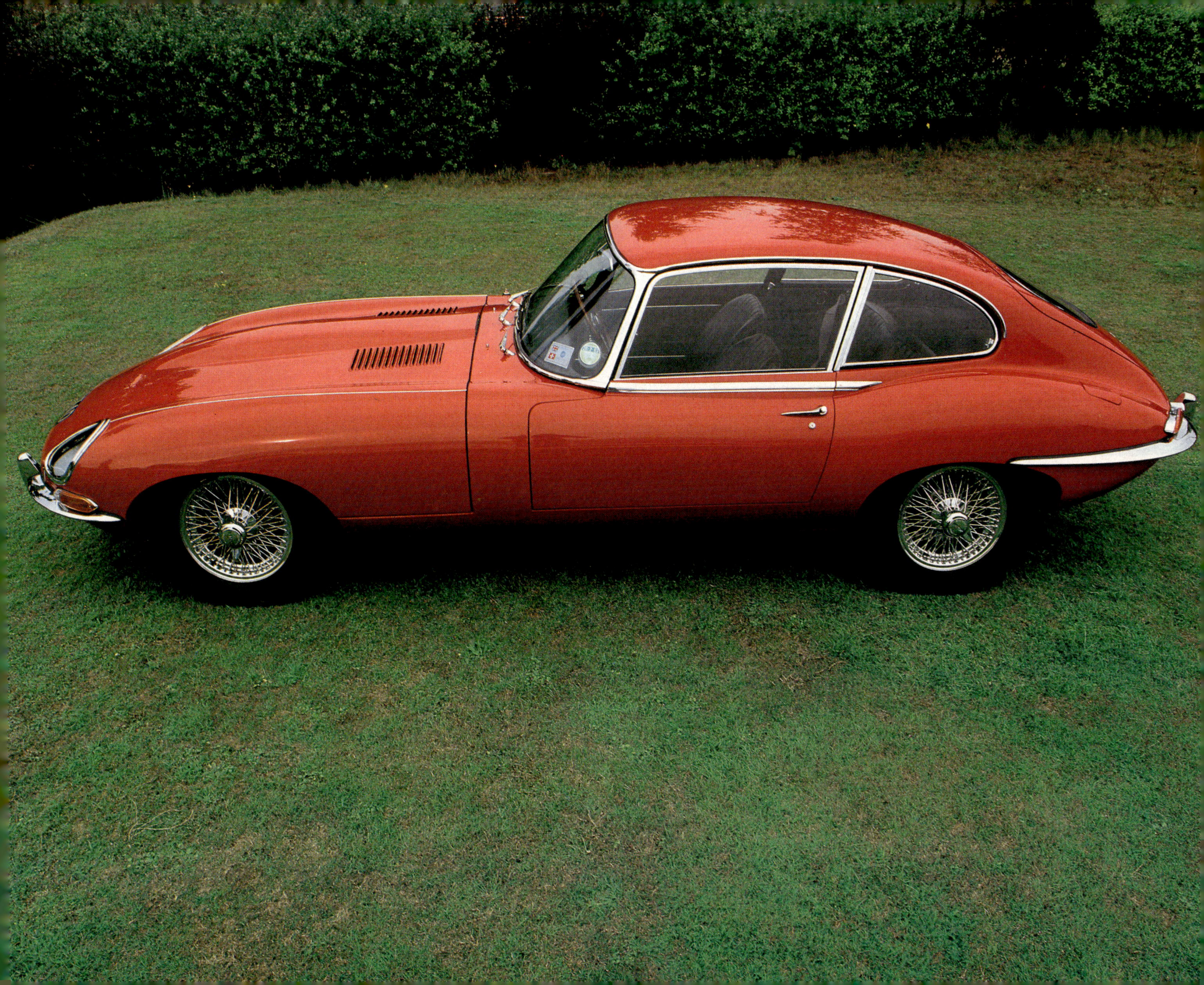

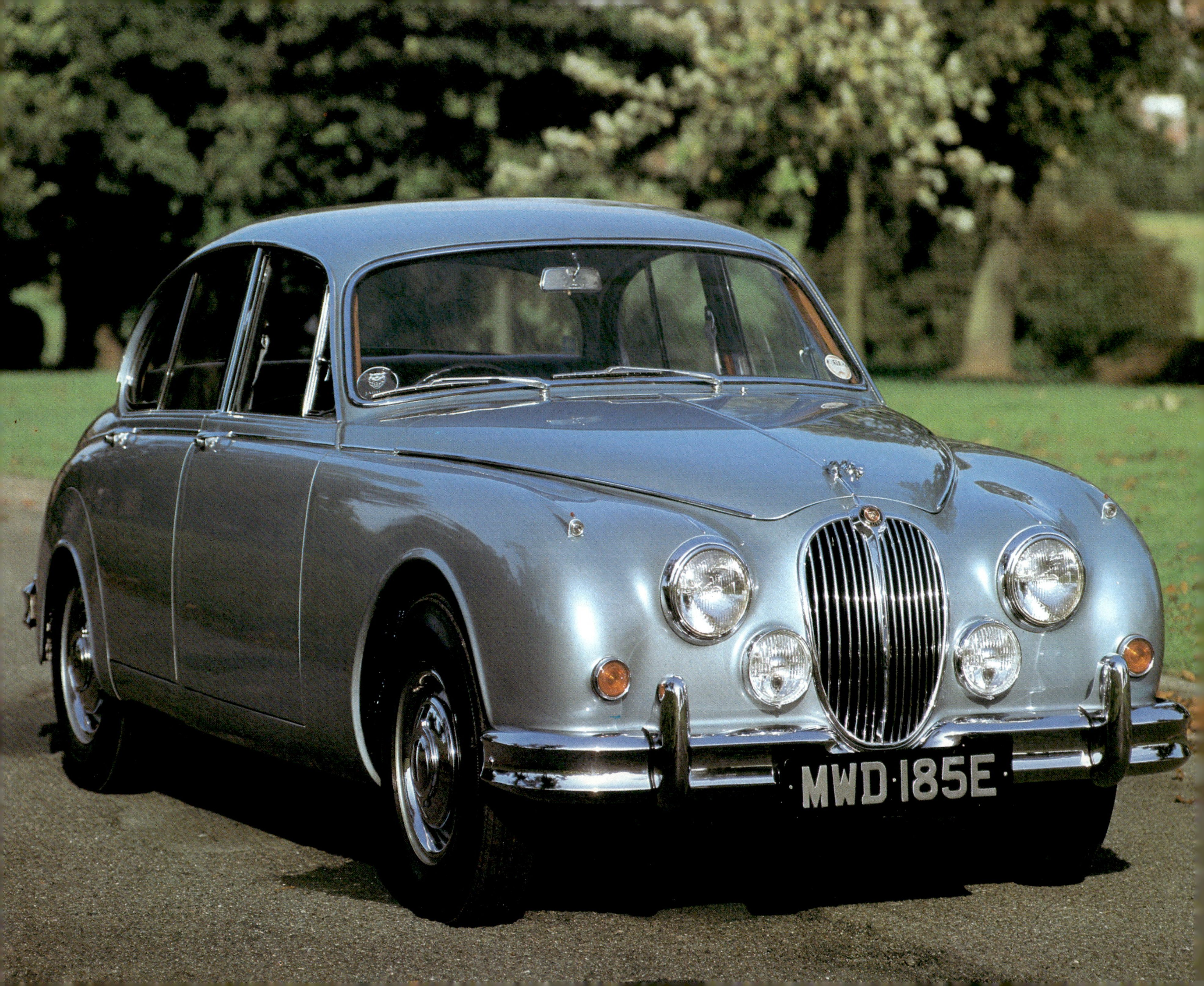
MWD·185E

To most Jaguar enthusiasts the timeless Mark II is the classic saloon. Introduced in 1959, the car was available with three different engine sizes: 2.4 litres, 3.4 litres and 3.8 litres, with the largest version giving a top speed of 125 mph. The Mark II remained in production until 1967. Illustrated is the 1967 2.4 version.

These pages: the Lindner-Nöcker E type, specially prepared for competition with a modified lightweight aluminium shell, was one of the fastest and most successful 6 cylinder racing versions of the car.

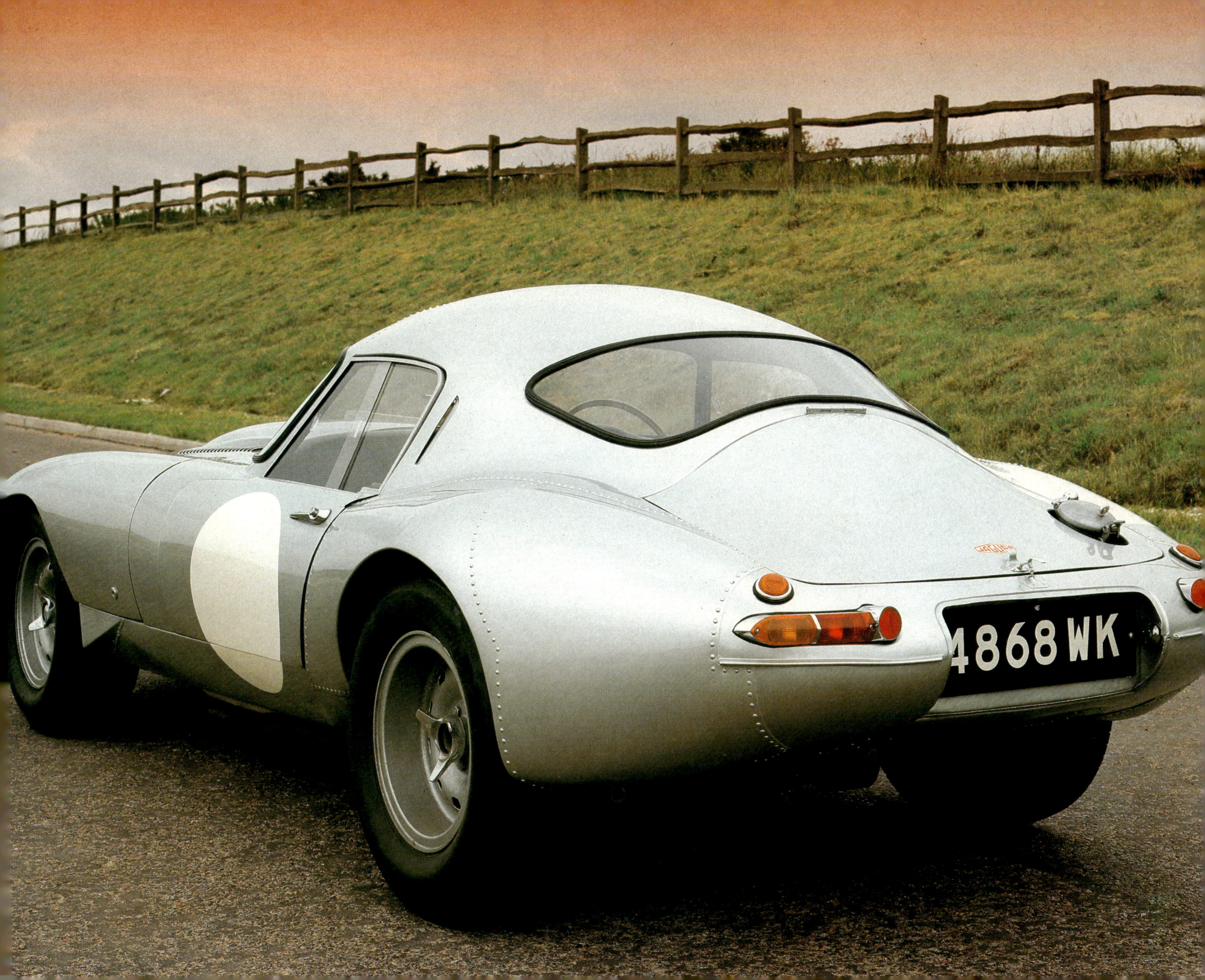
4868 WK

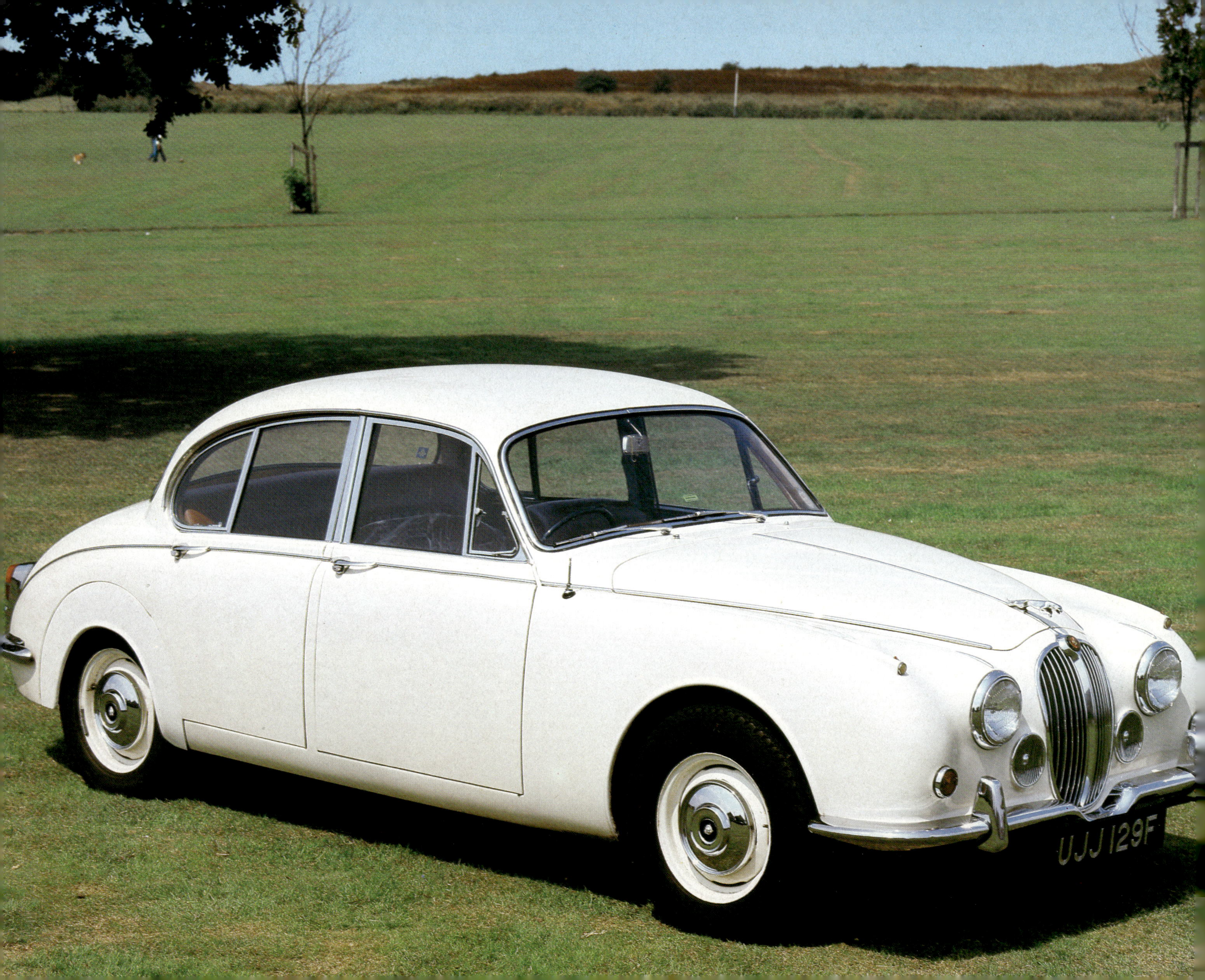
UJJ 129F

With the exception of the XJ6, the Mark II *these pages* was the most successful of the Jaguar saloon cars, both in terms of sales and performance. Outwardly similar to its predecessor the Mark I, the car was nevertheless a completely new model with drastically updated interior finish. Least exciting of the three engine versions available was the 2.4 litre, which, although it had an output of 120 bhp as opposed to the Mark I's 112 bhp, was somewhat slower due to increased weight. With a top speed of 93 mph, it was passed over by many enthusiastic motorists who preferred the considerably more lively 3.4 and 3.8 litre alternatives.

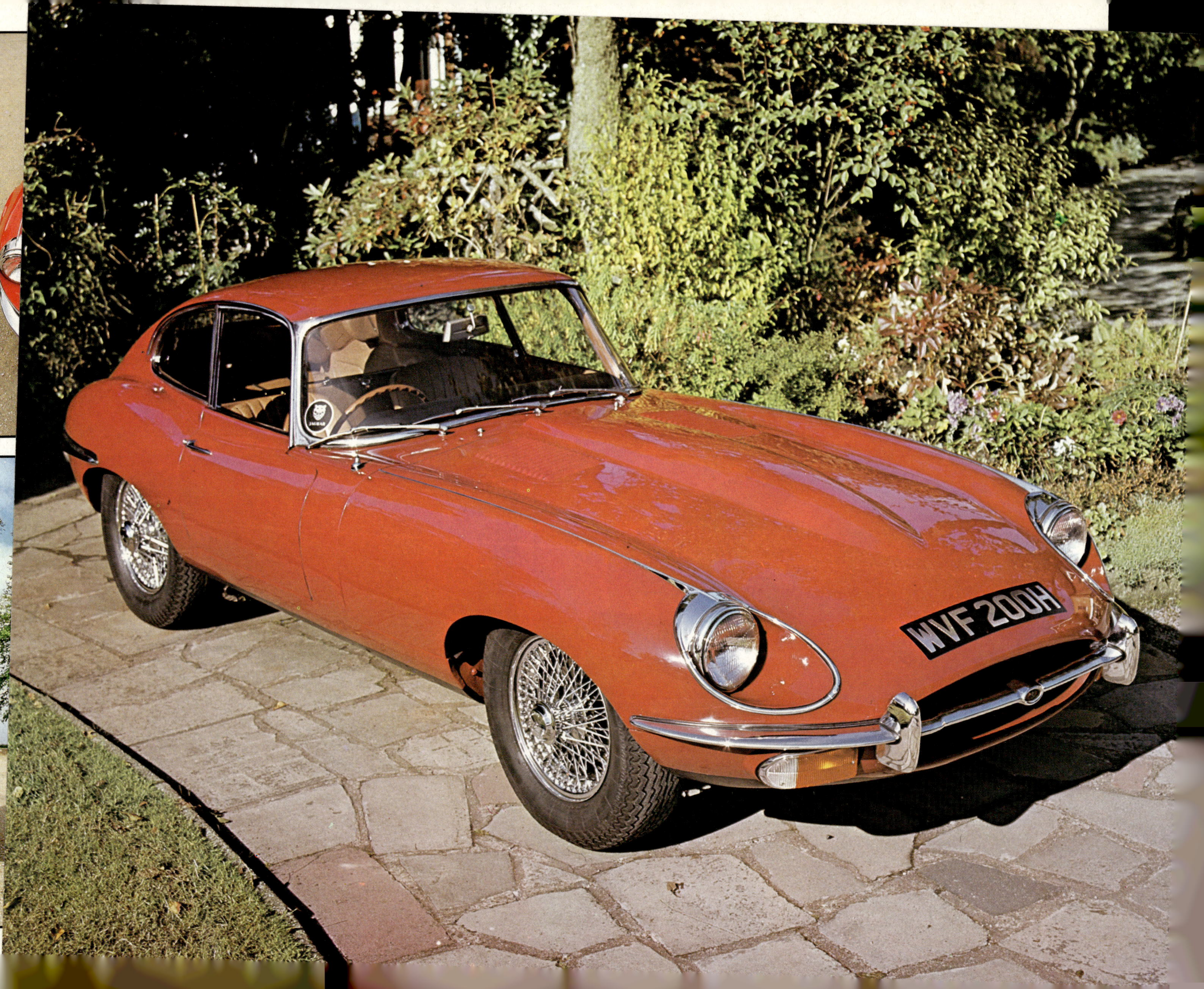
WVF 200H

1968 saw the introduction of the series 2 E type *these pages*. Apart from the cosmetic changes, such as the open headlights, the car also featured a larger air-intake which was necessary to cope with the higher running temperatures caused by extensive pollution modification for the American market. The top speed of the car, at 135 mph, was some 15 mph slower than on 1961 models.

Along with the new engine, the series 3 E type also sported the longer wheelbase that had been a feature of the 2+2. The air intake was once again enlarged, brakes were improved and wheel-arches became flared to accommodate the wider wheels. Power assisted steering was introduced to cope with the extra weight of the V 12 engine and cockpit space was increased. On the roadster model *these pages* a new hardtop was offered.

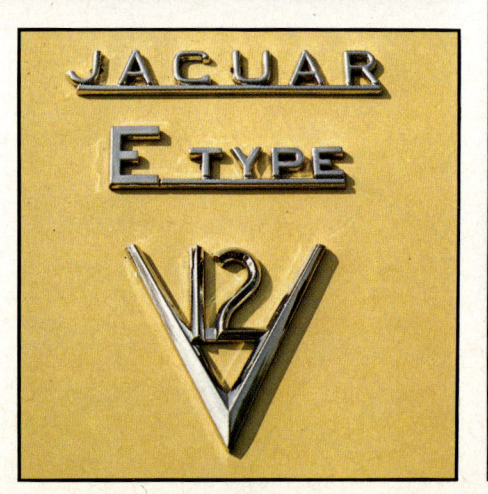

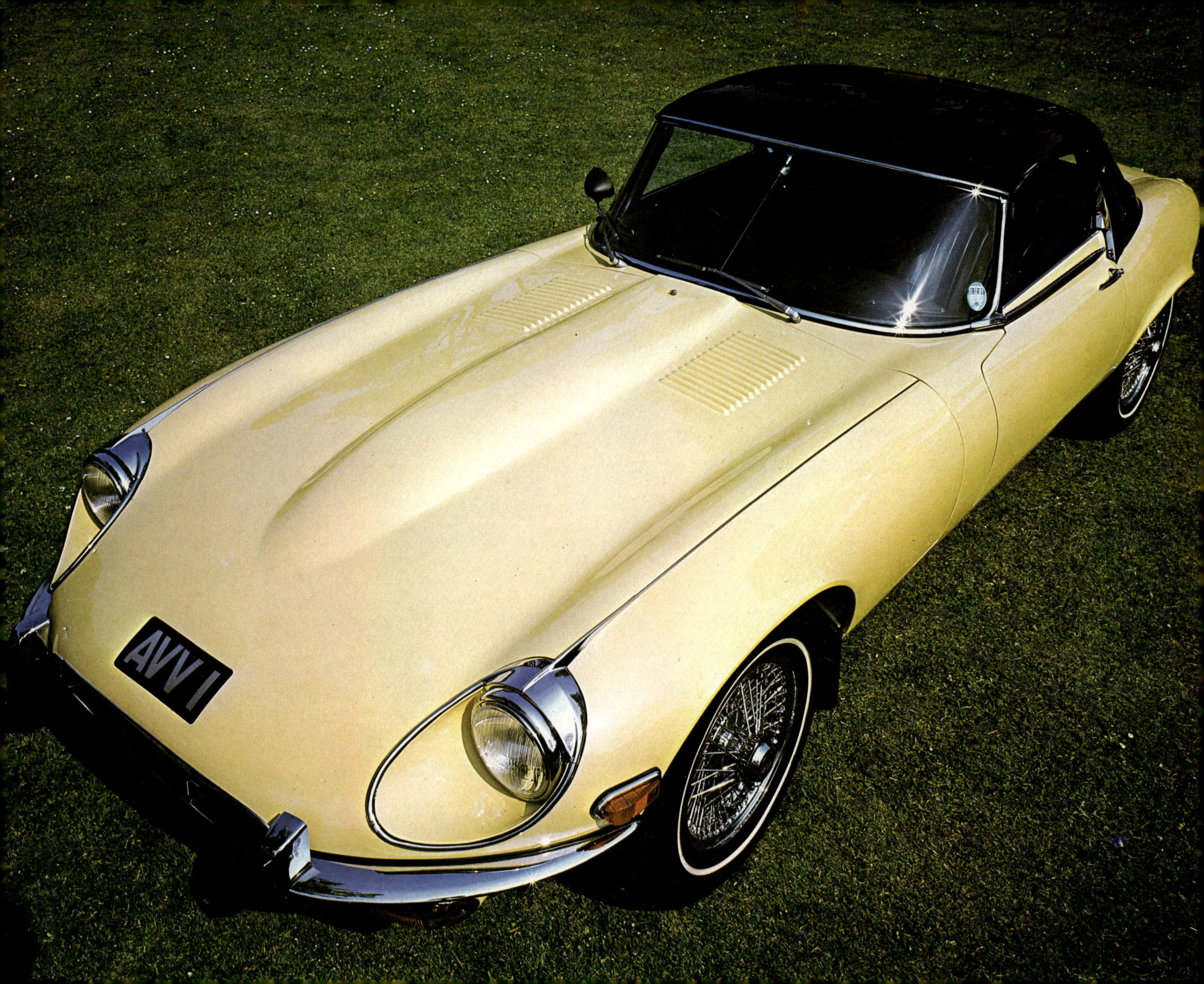
AVV 1

LUCAS
AMPS
C
D
FUEL
E 1/4 1/2 3/4 F
LIGHTS
OIL
20 40 60
WATER
INTERIOR MAP
PANEL
FAN
IGNITION
CIGAR
STARTER
FUEL
WIPER
WASHER
OFF
HEAT
AIR

The 420G *these pages* was to all intents and purposes a moderately revised version of the luxurious Mark X which had been introduced onto the market in the same year as the E type. Despite its considerable weight, length and width the 420G could outperform many lighter sportscars.

Based on both the 420 and the 420G, the XJ6 *these pages* was highly acclaimed by the press when it appeared in 1968. Available with either 4.2 litre or a new 2.8 litre engine, the car set new standards in handling comfort and silence that were to make it the most important saloon made by Jaguar to date. Sales of the new car reached a record of 32,000 in 1970.

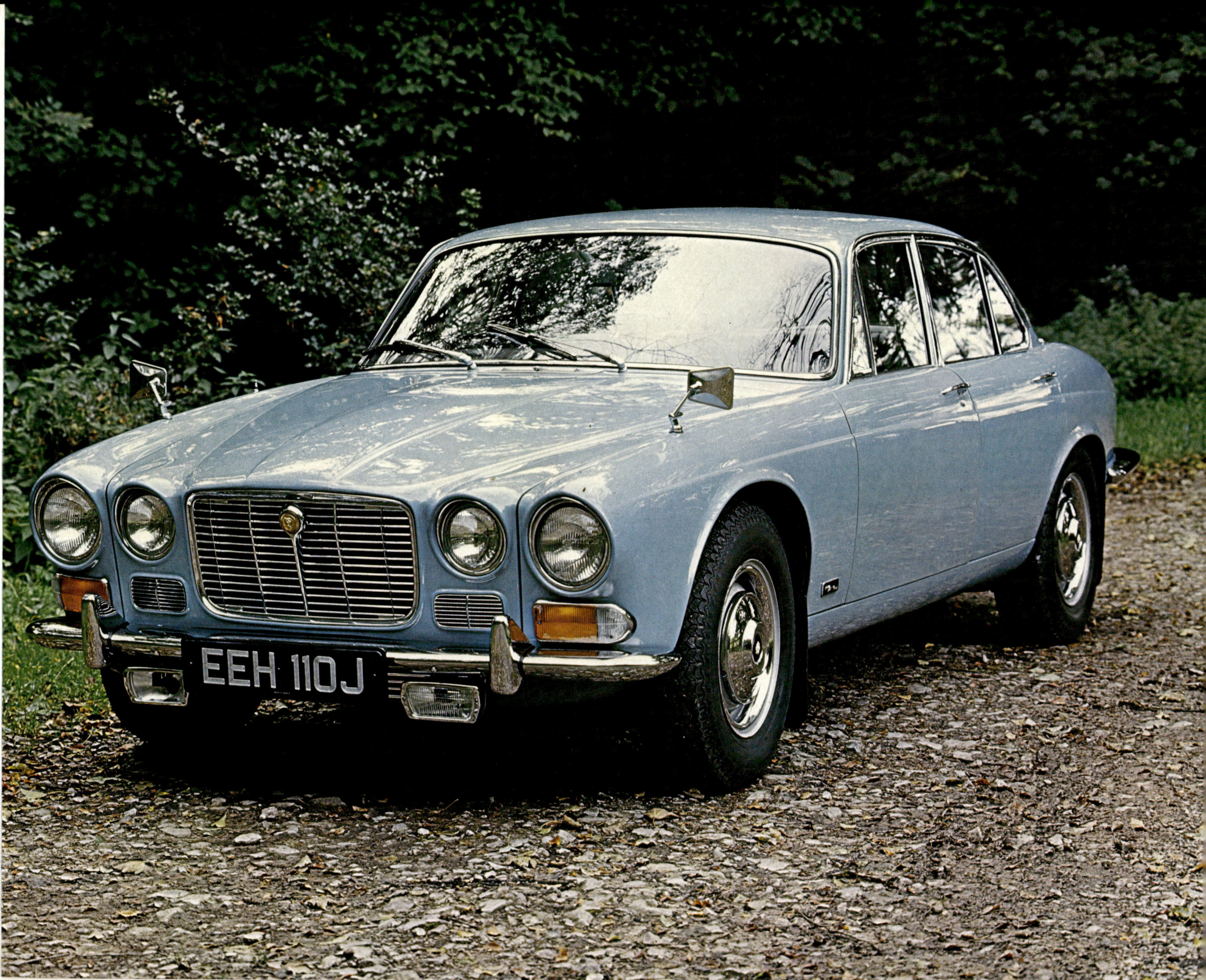
EEH 110J

The Lynx Eventer *these pages*, based on the XJS HE, combines the practical appeal of the estate car with the luxury that has come to be expected of the Jaguar. The high efficiency cylinder head that had been developed for the 12 cylinder engine gave a dramatic improvement in fuel consumption figures and increased performance still further in what was already a 150 mph car.

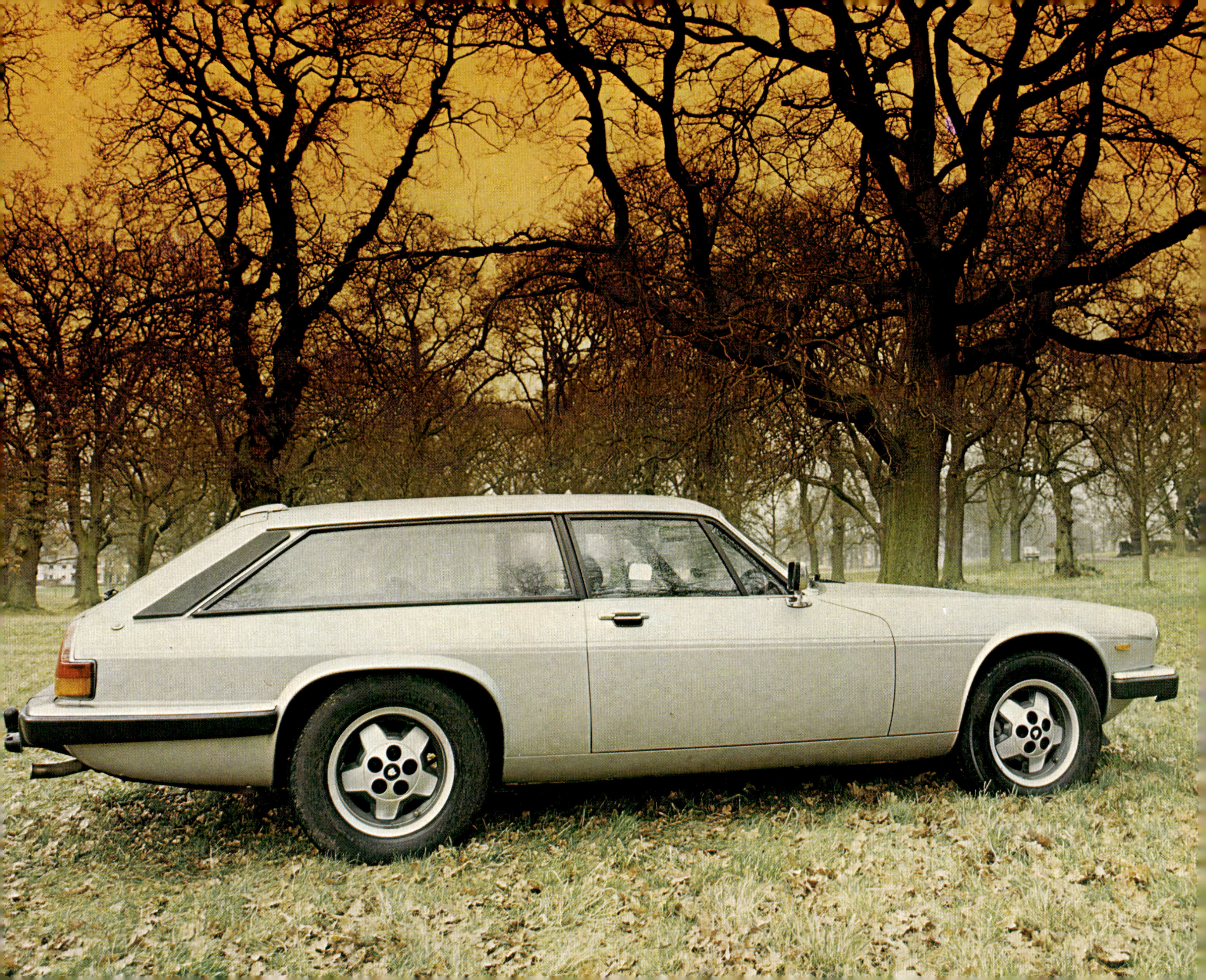

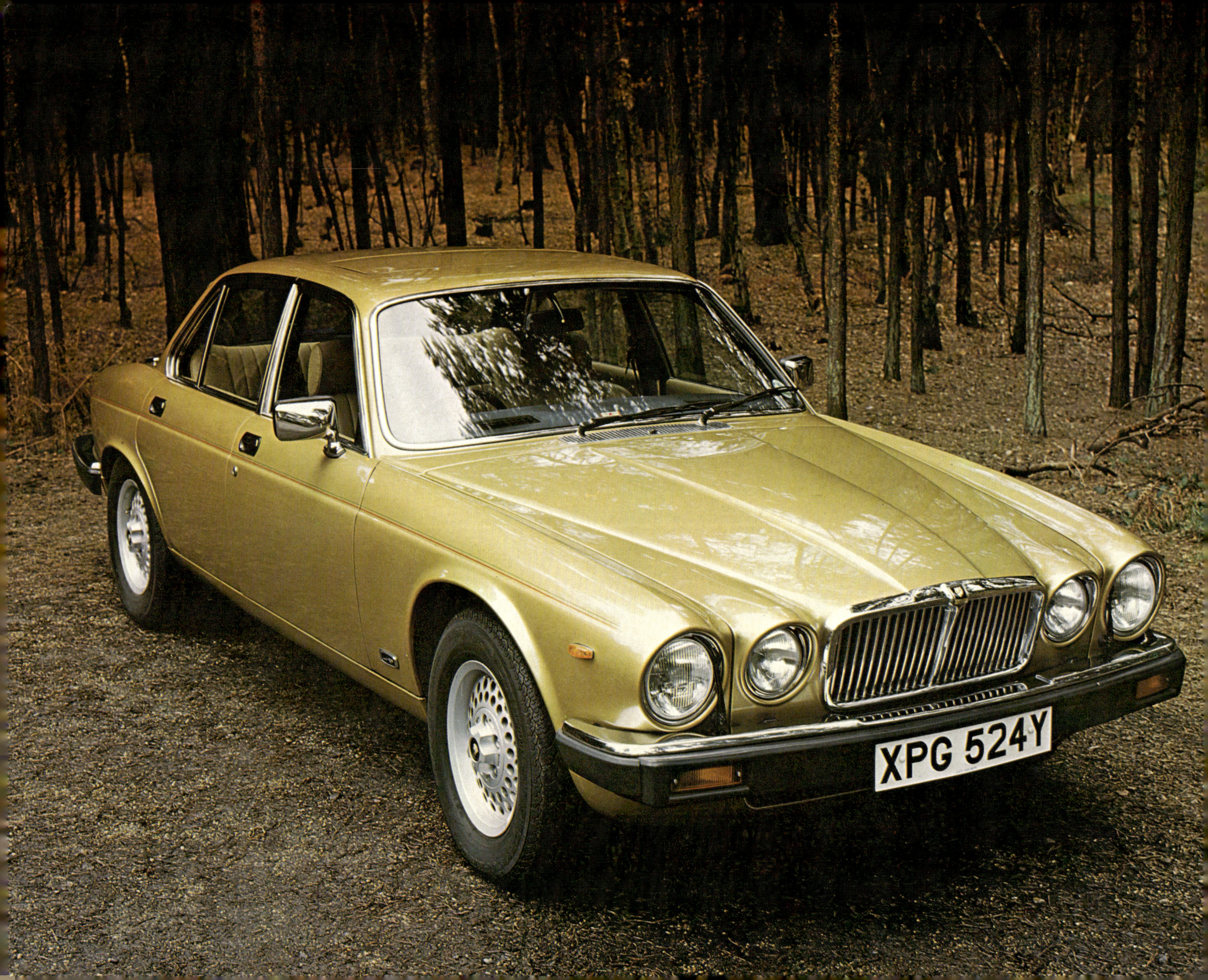
XPG 524Y

Latest in the line of luxury XJ saloons is the superb XJ12 *these pages*. The car shares the same 5.3 litre V-12 engine as the more sporty two-door XJS. Fuel economy is considered sufficiently important, even at the luxury end of the car market, for Jaguar to have developed their much-lauded high efficiency engine.

Designed by Lyons and Sayer, the 2+2 XJS is as much a Jaguar as any of its antecedents. Introduced in 1975, the car is available only as a fixed head coupé. The open version *above* is the special Spyder conversion by the firm of Lynx Engineering. Like its sporting predecessors, the XJS has been adapted for racing and continues to fare well, on American tracks in particular.

Copyright ©1988 by Colour Library Books Ltd.,
Guildford, Surrey, England.
First published in USA 1988
by Exeter Books
Distributed by Bookthrift
Exeter is a trademark of Bookthrift Marketing, Inc.
Bookthrift is a registered trademark of Bookthrift Marketing, Inc.
New York, New York

All rights reserved

ISBN 0-671-09396-7

Printed in Spain by Cronion, S.A.